Anything is Possible

Using the Power of Vision to Drive Innovation in Distribution

by
Dirk Beveridge

Copyright © 2016 Beveridge Business Systems

All rights reserved.

ISBN-10: 1539873099
ISBN-13: 978-1539873099

Contents

	Introduction	i
1	The Innovation Inversion Rule	1
2	The Power of Vision: Possibilities in Wholesale Distribution	7
3	Innovation is Bypassing Distribution	19
4	Introducing the Innovative Distributor™	23
5	How to Navigate to a Not So Distant Future	25
6	Distributors Have to Dream the Dream Again	31
7	Catalyze Change with The Visioning Spectrum: Anything is Possible!	35
8	Peering Into the Future	39
9	Next Steps to Unleashing the Power Behind YOUR Vision	43
	About the Author	47

Introduction

Do you believe that anything is possible?

Dirk Beveridge certainly does. He's convinced that distributors need to inject an "Anything is Possible" mindset into their business as a new mantra while inspiring a new spirit of innovation. In this first of a five-part essay series, Dirk shares why it's so important that each and every distributor understand that anything is possible - through the power of vision.

Dirk makes a strong case that without vision, there is no innovation. In today's age of rapid, foundational and disruptive change, leaders at every level of the organization must be able to articulate and communicate their vision of tomorrow. That future reality you really believe is possible... with committed effort.

In this inspiring essay, Dirk weaves a compelling story of related lessons from highly innovative businesses – from within distribution and beyond – and shows how you can peer into the future to eliminate ambiguity. He then provides specifics steps that you can craft and articulate your vision with the understanding ... that the only limits are your imagination and creativity.

After all ... Anything Is Possible.

ANYTHING IS POSSIBLE

Chapter 1
The Innovation Inversion Rule

Innovation is a vital exercise for even the most successful businesses, so let's start with this great illustration through a story I want to share with you about Robert Goizueta from Coca-Cola. Some years ago, Roberto Goizueta, Coca-Cola's CEO at the time, was evaluating the organization, and found that, not surprisingly, they had a 47% share of the market. Basically it controlled half the market. But he also found that this success had created a problem: Complacency.

You see, when a company is thriving and massively profitable, there's a natural tendency to be drawn towards the status quo. Companies tend to get very comfortable with the way things are. After all, if things are working extremely well, why change anything? As a consequence, however, almost no thought is given to innovation when a company is thriving. This phenomenon is called The Innovation Inversion Rule.

The Innovation Inversion Rule states that **the urgency of innovation and the ability to innovate are inversely related**. In other words, when a company is most able to innovate, generally innovation is the last thing on its mind. In the case of Coca-Cola for example, it certainly had the ability, the talent, the brand, and the financial resources to innovate. What was missing, though, was the motivation and a sense of urgency precisely because they were already so successful.

We see the Innovation Inversion Rule play itself out in business all the time. I've even seen it questioned first-hand specifically within the wholesale distribution industry itself. A couple of years ago, the National Association of Wholesaler-Distributors asked me to conduct the first and only research project on the state of innovation throughout **distribution**. This led to the creation of my book, *INNOVATE! How Successful Distributors Lead Change in Disruptive Times*.

Now here's where this lesson really hit home for me: After compiling all of this research into actionable insights on how to innovate, I was excited to get the book into the hands of ambitious distributors, believing that the information contained within would change how they conducted their businesses. However, I was surprised and even a bit dismayed when I received an email from my publisher asking me if, before we went to print, we should address whether this is an important enough topic to get out to the marketplace.

Remember, this was a national association representing all wholesale distributors. Even they were asking, "Why should distributors run their business any differently if their current model is working well and they're profitable?" Even here, in an organization tasked with informing distributors and keeping them on the cutting edge, there was a bias against innovation when things are going well.

Think about the tendency toward the status quo in your own organization and in the meetings that you've been in. Too often we see that suggestions of an innovation or change to move the company forward are met with reluctance simply because what the company was doing at the time was already working for them. These situations are examples of the urgency of innovation and the ability to innovate being inversely related.

Great leaders aren't satisfied with the status quo. To continue our Coca-Cola story, although Roberto Goizueta was aware that his company had 47% share of the marketplace, he was concerned about complacency. Looking around his company, he saw that the business had settled into a comfortable status quo. He saw everything within the organization *except for innovation*. He knew his company had the ability to innovate but, at the same time, he saw that the urgency was lacking. So what did he do?

Because Mr. Goizueta didn't have all the answers himself, he brought in subject matter experts to help rethink the business, and he learned that he was looking at things the wrong way. Rather than just focusing on Coca-Cola's success and 47% market share, he began thinking about other numbers as well. He thought about how, at the time, there were 5.7 billion people on planet earth. In order to survive, each one of those people needed to drink an average of 64 ounces of fluid per day. 5.7 billion people multiplied by the 64 ounces they drink on a daily basis means that almost three billion gallons of fluid were being consumed each day!

This shift in thinking led Goizueta to the realization that Coca-Cola didn't have a 47% share of the market, but instead a 47% share of *only the soft drink market*. When it came to the total fluids consumed, Coca-Cola actually had less than a 2% market share!

His change of perspective helped him craft a new vision for Coca-Cola and its employees, which included growing their market share. Before that day, employees looked at the 47% number and said, "What else do you want us to do? We've got all the business we can get. How can we possibly grow our market share further?" However, with this new information in mind, Coca-Cola employees began to think differently. They saw that there was a large, untapped market ripe for growth. The new thinking led to a wave of innovation and strategic partnerships that helped grow the business.

Of course, in order to drive that growth and vision, Goizueta had to work hard to change the frame of reference for not only his leadership team but the entire organization. Getting employees to think about Coca-Cola's share of the overall market of billions of gallons of fluid consumed each day, rather than the 47% share among soft drinks, was a great start.

Why was all this so important? Goizueta understood that the status quo, the current thinking that helped Coca-Cola become successful at the time, wasn't necessarily going to be what moved the organization forward, or ensured prosperity in the years to come. He needed his employees to challenge their current assumptions and question their worldview. Were they in the soft drink business? Or were they in the fluid consumption business? Once Coca-Cola employees moved past seeing themselves as only a soft drink company, they acquired a new vision allowing them to see that anything was possible.

ANYTHING IS POSSIBLE

Chapter 2
The Power of Vision -- Possibilities in Wholesale Distribution

When we change our frame of reference, inject new thinking, and question current assumptions, anything is possible. It's what gives us the vision to land a man on the moon and return him safely to earth afterward. It's what gives us the vision to realize that driverless cars are possible. Even drone deliveries – the stuff of science fiction just a few years ago – are now becoming commonplace because of the power of a greater vision.

When the power of vision is applied to business, it helps us create new business models, value propositions, and customer experiences. For instance, when Howard Schultz was in Europe, he saw how Europeans jumped from coffee shop to coffee shop. It gave him a new frame of reference and inspired a new vision for him -- to create a coffee shop that was more than just a coffee shop, but a third essential place in our lives. As a result, today, we have home, we have work, and – for many of us – that third essential place is Starbucks.

When I consider how anything is possible through the power of vision, I can't help but think of the amazing potential and importance of wholesale distribution. Today there are plenty of reasons to be excited when it comes to wholesale distribution. There are somewhere between 250,000 to 300,000 businesses throughout the distribution industry. These businesses range anywhere from pure entrepreneurial businesses to Fortune 500 businesses. Distribution is a massive 5 to 8 trillion-dollar industry employing roughly 5.9 million people.

Think about those numbers! The auto industry – which is currently inventing driverless cars – is "only" a $900 billion industry, and here we are at 5 to 8 trillion dollars. The soft drink industry is "only" $98 billion. In fact, wholesale distribution represents 6% of the overall U.S. economy. It's absolutely integral to manufacturing, retail, health care and other sectors of the supply chain.

When I take a look at wholesale distribution, I truly believe that anything is possible. Yet, while anything is possible in distribution, my research shows that 72% of wholesale distribution leaders believe that the pace of change is too slow in their business. And, 85% of wholesale distribution leaders believe that much of the industry is operating from a dated business model. So, while anything is possible, we also see that innovation is lagging. Change and transformation are lagging.

As we saw with the Coca-Cola example, when we change our frame of reference and look at our businesses in a completely new way, anything is possible; so clearly we need to change our frame of reference in order to innovate. This isn't just true for Coca-Cola, Amazon, Tesla, and the other companies that make news headlines. This is also true for you, whether you're an entrepreneurial distributor or a Fortune 500 distributor.

It doesn't matter if you're a brick and mortar distributor or exclusively e-commerce. It doesn't matter if you're a functional line manager or whether you're in operations, administration, or sales. When we change our frame of reference, anything is possible.

Here are three examples of distributors who changed their frames of reference, which also changed the results they've achieved.

 The first example is Berlin Packaging, a national organization headquartered in the Chicago area. Berlin is in the rigid packaging business. They distribute caps, bottles, closures and items of that nature.

Over the last 20 years, Berlin has experienced double digit growth while their competitors are only growing at 2 to 3%. How do they drive that growth? It starts with the part of their vision that says, "We will become indispensable to our customers."

Berlin Packaging has a bold vision which has translated into an incredible reality. It's led the company consistently driving absolutely outstanding results.

For Berlin Packaging, a large part of this strategy involves having employees who can share and help to drive the company's vision. Having a team on the same page is important because you can't do it alone. An outstanding team can help to drive your company's vision in astounding ways.

Even when interviewing new candidates for hire, Berlin will share their vision with the candidates and ask them if they want to be part of that vision and to share in imagining what the company could become by challenging the status quo and daring to do something different. This vision isn't something that every candidate could get on-board with but the ones who share those ideals help to drive the company forward.

The ideals that Berlin chose to embody and the vision they had involved re-framing their perspective away from merely selling customers a product to thinking about how their product could enrich their customers' lives.

 The second example, U.S. LBM, is in the building materials industry. They've gone from an idea on a napkin in 2009 – back when the company didn't even exist – to becoming a $2 billion distributor in just seven years. Part of their vision was to create a company that would change the building materials distribution industry.

This vision led to the creation of a culture that wasn't afraid of change and wasn't held back by a fear of failure. L.T. Gibson, the company's president and CEO, credits much of U.S. LBM's success to this vision and the culture it created.

"Vision almost creates a safety net that allows change to occur," Gibson has said. "Without change, you obviously can't have innovation. The two are so connected. You have to communicate a vision to your people so they know why the company is changing and what's being changed. This allows the changes to happen at a faster rate. When employees can see exactly what the vision of a company is, the day-to-day decisions become very easy because they can evaluate each decision in terms of whether or not it's consistent with the company's vision."

So you see here that vision can be an incredible tool when it comes to motivating and encouraging teams, especially because it helps employees overcome their natural fear of failure.

U.S. LBM goes to great lengths to drive the fear of failure from employees through training and classes. It's a necessary exercise because a fear of failure holds people back from taking the risks that can help to grow the organization.

When you take risks, you will occasionally fail. Albert Einstein is famously quoted as saying, "A person who never made a mistake never tried anything new." To grow and succeed, both businesses and people have to try new things.

> *"I think the most important job of a leader, of any business and at any level, is to communicate the company's vision to their people."*
>
> ~ L.T. Gibson, U.S. LBM

Only after banishing fear from your organization will your associates feel fully confident when it comes to making decisions and fully engaging in your company's vision.

The key to success for U.S. LBM was getting all hands on deck. Rather than relying solely on seasoned leaders with decades of experience under their belt – who could be a few years from retirement – their approach was to ensure that people at all levels were involved in driving U.S. LBM's success. This meant getting everybody involved in the company's vision.

Remember, U.S. LBM's vision wasn't merely to succeed, but instead to change the industry. By pursuing this bold vision and getting everybody in the organization on-board, U.S. LBM has achieved the kind of success that most distributors only dream about.

The final example is APR Supply, a phenomenal organization led by Scott Weaver, which has managed to consistently double its sales every five years. Believe it or not, doubling sales is part of the company's vision. APR Supply is committed to developing leaders who will eventually have the capability to become presidents of their own companies.

How has APR Supply managed these incredible feats? In short, their vision has helped to make it a "future-oriented" company. Weaver and his team plan five years in advance which, in turn, has helped them double their revenue every five years.

In fact, at APR Supply, they use a five-year time horizon because they think that the world is changing too quickly to look ahead 10 years. Their vision includes what they should be doing and how they should be acting, in addition to looking at the number of associates, locations, and so on, to help them determine what they should look like as an organization five years from now.

They hold quarterly meetings every year to determine what needs to be done during that year to help them reach their five-year vision. In these meetings they discuss how to make themselves and their teams better, and they spend time working ON the business rather than IN the business.

Their goal is to double the size of their business every five years, and as a part of this process, they know they need new leaders and new people who they can promote.

This idea of preparing for the future represents the incredible vision and planning that goes on at APR Supply. This foresight and attention to detail has helped to make the company's vision of doubling its sales every five years a reality.

~~

Once again, these examples demonstrate how anything is possible once you change your frame of reference and look at things in a different light.

There are a number of practices that you can start undertaking today to change your own frame of reference in order to craft a new vision for your organization. Here are four practices to get you started.

Practice #1: Be Hungry and Humble

This first practice involves adopting a different mindset. The most innovative, most visionary, and boldest thinkers I know are both humble *and* hungry. They want growth, they want to achieve excellence, and they want to dominate. They are often pleased, but they are never satisfied. In fact, the best innovators I know have ambition and a strong point of view, but they're also surprisingly humble. They know that they don't have all the answers. They recognize their own shortcomings, and they are willing to consider new ideas that others suggest.

All too often leadership can stifle innovation and transformation efforts, especially when those in leadership positions believe that they're solely responsible for coming up with and implementing new ideas. Innovation is a team effort. You will not and, frankly, cannot have all the answers. This is why it's important to rely on others in your organization as well. Be curious about other people's points of view, and be willing to hear and consider those opinions even when they conflict with your own. Explore and acknowledge these points of view because they very well may reveal something that you've missed. Anything is possible when you bring humility and hunger into the business.

Practice #2: Look for Ideas Outside of the Distribution Industry

The second practice involves looking outside of our industry for ideas and answers. For the most part, companies in the distribution industry have been one-dimensional and inward-looking. For years, we've hung out with and learned from the same types of businesses, the same organizations, and maintained the same relationships. The industry as a whole has been very insular, and this has led to serious ideological stagnation.

The solutions to the significant opportunities and

challenges that we face in distribution will not be found within distribution. Instead, we have to look outside our industry. There's an entire world of innovators outside of our circle. There are entirely new business models and cultures being developed outside of the distribution world. To find new ideas and truly innovate, we have to look outside of our concentric circle to that outside world.

Everyone knows that one of the foremost innovators of our age was Steve Jobs. We can learn so much from him! One of the things he said that has most impacted my career – and I deeply believe to be true – is, "It comes down to trying to expose yourself to the best that humans have done. And then try to bring those things into what you're doing."

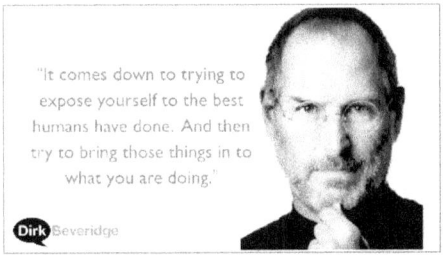

Jobs's words emphasize the importance of a broad approach. After all, he didn't say it comes down to trying to expose yourself to the best that other *distributors* have done. He didn't say to L.T. Gibson at U.S. LBM that it comes down to trying to expose yourself to the best that other building materials distributors have done. He didn't say to Andrew Berlin that it comes down to trying to expose yourself to the best that other rigid packaging distributors have done. He didn't say to Scott Weaver that it comes down to trying to expose yourself to the best that other plumbing distributors have done. He said that it comes down to exposing yourself to the best that humans have done and then bringing those things into what you're doing in your own business. Anything is possible once you start looking outside of our industry for new ideas and to change your frame of reference.

Practice #3: Move Beyond Your Current Network

The third practice involves thinking about how you can move beyond your current network. As distributors, we have amazing relationships where we help one another. Through these relationships and networks, we've exchanged many of our best practices, and we've realized some pretty great successes.

However, innovation requires moving from "best" practices to "next" practices. It involves meeting new people and expanding beyond only learning from those close-knit groups or relationships that you've probably built your career on. What you've done over the years may be good or even great, but it can be better!

What we've traditionally done with our network of individuals within the industry is go to councils and meetings, and have lunches together where we share best practices then race back to our organizations to implement the best of those practices that we aren't currently using. Ultimately, this drives parity and sameness within the industry.

Innovators aren't satisfied with parity; nor are they satisfied with sameness. They're driven by a need to break through that status quo. You can break

> "The future is already here -- it's just not evenly distributed."
>
> ~ William Gibson

through it yourself quite simply by expanding your network; because once you get outside of your current network of relationships, you very well may find new practices which far exceed your current best practices as well as new ideas that can power your business. New networks can help you find new technology, models, cultures, and value propositions. You'll find the *next* practices rather than just the same best practices circulating around your industry because anything is possible when you move beyond your current networks.

Practice #4: Explore the Future

The fourth practice that will change your frame of reference involves exploring the future. As distributors, we <u>must</u> explore the future. I love the following quote from William Gibson: "The future is already here – it's just not evenly distributed." Consider those words carefully. Every day there are things happening outside of your awareness. New trends are impacting businesses and other industries beyond yours that are already changing the way your customers do business. It's changing your customers' expectations and demands and affecting what they look for from their suppliers, vendors, and partners.

The future is all around us, and it's possible to see emerging trends before they become an industry standard. As such, we must explore the future. We need to peer into it to see where the market, industry, and economy are going so that we can ensure that we'll be ahead of that curve.

Personally, I try to engage in these exact four practices – which I think are critical for everybody in my organization – <u>on a daily basis</u>. Thinking about how those four practices have changed my frame of reference brings to mind the following story about how my own status quo was disrupted.

ANYTHING IS POSSIBLE

Chapter 3
Innovation is Bypassing Distribution

Around five years ago, the Secretary of Defense invited me, along with 39 other individuals from across the country, to spend a week learning about the U.S. military. The entire week-long experience was, in a word, amazing.

We started in the Pentagon before traveling down to Guantanamo Bay, flew to Rio de Janeiro, and then visited the U.S.S. George Washington in the middle of the Atlantic. Next, we traveled to Colombia where we spent two days out in the jungle with the U.S. special operation forces and the Colombian special operation forces. We then visited Honduras where we saw how the military was developing partnerships by building schools and delivering soccer balls. Finally, we spent a day in Key West with the Coast Guard.

I tell this story partly because it's one of the reasons this essay exists. You see, when I was on the deck of the U.S.S. George Washington, through serendipity – and because I was willing to put myself in a new situation – I met a gentleman by the name of Saul Kaplan.

Saul lives in Providence, Rhode Island, and each year he hosts a conference called the Business Innovation Factory (BIF) summit. While we were chatting, He invited me to attend, so I flew out to Providence for two days where I listened to 30 storytellers who each gave a presentation lasting no longer than 20 minutes apiece. The presentations were more varied than I would ever have imagined.

For example, we heard from a social entrepreneur who talked about how their team innovated to help Hurricane Katrina victims, and we heard from the Vice President of Innovation for Intel, and we heard from just about every other industry and a myriad of people who fall in between the two. My mind felt like it was exploding with ideas listening to all of these stories. The one and only thing that the speakers had in common? "Innovation."

As I listened to these stories, I thought about my 25 years working with distributors; time I spent helping them drive customer-centricity and value added leadership throughout their sales organization. Then, as I was putting that experience together with all of these new ideas, it suddenly struck me that not once did any of the speakers talk about distribution; and yet, as I sat there listening, I was thinking about the 250,000 distributors in this country and what these messages on innovation would mean to them.

On the second day of the conference, while everyone was off to lunch, I found myself glued to my chair unable to move. I sat there reflecting about my lifetime in distribution and what I had learned over the past day and a half, when I had this tremendous "Aha" moment; and I jotted down a quick note to myself. On that note were four simple words that contained, for me, a profound meaning.

"Innovation is bypassing distribution."

I had started to connect the dots seeing how it all fit

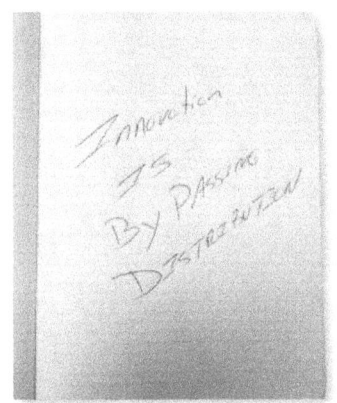

together, and it was that idea, that epiphany, that I brought back from Providence that day.

Right away I began calling every distribution company president and CEO that I knew to tell them about my epiphany. Many of them responded with, "Dirk, you're onto something. We definitely need a catalyst for change." These conversations then led to the creation of the UnleashWD Conference – an annual innovation summit created specifically for distributors.

Like the Business Innovation Factory, UnleashWD brings in the strategies and messages of the world's greatest leaders – all from outside of distribution – all thought disruptors and innovators from all different industries. It's exactly what the distribution industry needed to move forward.

Taking a cue from Saul Kaplan, we put these thought leaders on stage in front of distribution industry professionals to inject new thinking into our industry, changing our frames of reference, giving us new vision.

The information shared and connections made each year at UnleashWD are, in a word, unprecedented. This is probably the most powerful way I've ever seen to show distributors *how* anything is possible and *how* it starts with the power of vision and *how* we can change our frame of reference.

ANYTHING IS POSSIBLE

Chapter 4
Introducing the Innovative Distributor™

The UnleashWD Conference led to an important research project with the National Association of Wholesalers. The NAW recognized the need for new thinking, and they wanted to present their members with ways to drive innovation throughout our industry. The research we conducted helped us discover a new **model – The Innovative Distributor™**. It showed that if we're going to be relevant, and if we're going to be sustainable, we need to ingrain within our business the mindset that anything is possible. Through the research, we could clearly see that every distributor who strives for future success will become an innovative distributor. It's inevitable. They're

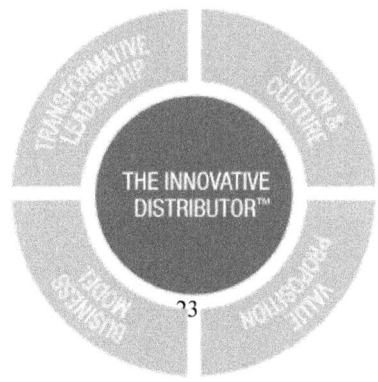

going to innovate around their vision. They're going to innovate around their cultures, value propositions, business models, and their companies' leadership.

Building upon this idea, we then began more groundbreaking research – this time with the National Association of Electrical Distributors. What we discovered through this project was that there exists a significant need to re-imagine and innovate around the partnerships between manufacturers and distributors. The results of the NAED research included the shocking revelation that 91% of distributors and manufacturers believe that the current model is broken, and there is a very clear need for a new frame of reference and innovation. There is a very clear need for change.

This call for change extends across the entire distribution industry. Remember: 85% of distributors believe that they're operating from an outdated business model, and 72% believe that the pace of change is too slow in their organizations. This tells us that innovation is sorely lacking. Often times, those data points can be traced back directly to the void of vision within a distributor's organization; because without vision, as I'm sure you're beginning to understand, there is no innovation.

ANYTHING IS POSSIBLE

Chapter 5
How to Navigate to a Not So Distant Future

What is vision, exactly? Vision is best defined as ***a future reality that we sincerely believe is possible with committed effort***. Vision is where we say to ourselves, "Here's where we are today as an organization. Here are our core competencies. Here's what we do very well. Here are the things that are driving our profitability. Here's what we do to create satisfied customers. We know that the world is changing. We know we have to think about disruption. We know that the future is going to be different… this means our business will and must be different."

Vision is the ability to craft, articulate, and communicate this future reality. It's not about where you are today, but rather what your organization will become. Vision is necessary to kick-start your innovation and change your efforts.

Two years ago, the Chief Sales Officer of Blinds.com, Steve Riddell, – who is an extremely brilliant leader – spoke at the UnleashWD Summit. His presentation drove home the idea of just how critical vision is when he reminded us that *what we want to become is far more important than our current state*. You already know what you are today. Your customers know what you are today. However, what makes you relevant today might not make you relevant or even profitable tomorrow.

It's vision that drives change, transformation, and innovation. It's vision that tells us that anything is possible. For another example within the distribution industry, let's turn back to U.S. LBM.

U.S. LBM was founded in 2009 by L.T. Gibson and a team of leaders in the building materials industry. If you were to look at the cover of ProSales magazine in May 2010, you'd see the headline, "Emerging Force: U.S. LBM may be the biggest dealer you never heard of. That won't last for long." The magazine was right because L.T. and his team had vision. They believed that anything was possible.

Fast forward to January 2015, and look at the new cover of that same magazine. Five years later, the reporting is that U.S. LBM has built itself into a $1.4 billion juggernaut; since then it's grown to over $2 billion today. How? It all started with their vision.

> *It's not about where you are today, but rather what your organization will become.*

I have a weekly podcast **called Innovate! for the Future.**

Every Monday the podcast, which is available on iTunes, features a new episode filled with inspirational stories of how leaders within distribution and beyond are innovating and creating new opportunities for their businesses. In an early episode titled "Setting Out to Change an Industry – The Power of Vision," I interviewed L.T. Gibson, and we discussed the importance of vision.

L.T. Gibson set out to change an industry. During that podcast, he explained, "It's so hard for a lot of distributors to think about changing the industry because they come up through the process and they really don't want to change the industry." They're being pulled back to the status quo.

However, U.S. LBM and L.T. Gibson are different because L.T. and his team believed and continue to believe that anything is possible at U.S. LBM. And, that belief begins and ends with their customers. Remember the story of Coca-Cola? How, instead of looking at their 47% soft drink market share, the company began looking at the massive number of ounces of fluid consumed per day by 5.8 billion people on the planet which gave Coca-Cola a less than 2% market share? At U.S. LBM, they had to change their frame of reference as well.

So, U.S. LBM gathered data points by talking to their customers and saw that their customers and the industry had accepted business being done one way. The scheduling of projects, crews, and deliveries was always difficult. There was always product shrinkage at the job sites and a lot of redundancy in job cost. Then there were issues with telephone tag. When a contractor at the job site didn't have his materials, he'd call his outside sales representatives to ask, "Hey, where's my product?" The outside sales representative would reply, "I don't know. Let me find out." He, in turn, calls the branch manager and the operations manager to ask them, "Hey, where's Joe's product?" The operations manager says, "I don't know. I'll get back to you," before calling the driver. There are four or five calls to get that one simple answer, and then another four or five calls would be made to get that answer all the way back to that contractor.

> *What makes you relevant today might not make you relevant or even profitable tomorrow.*

The industry had accepted the telephone tag issue as an inescapable reality. Nobody wanted to attack the problem. Nobody wanted to rethink it until U.S. LBM said, "Let's change our frame of reference and find a way to innovate around those challenges."

Again, they looked to the thinking of Steve Jobs. They didn't look within building materials or even within distribution. Instead, they looked outside of distribution. They looked outside because they wanted to find the best that humans have done and shift it into their business. They wanted to go beyond the best practices that all building materials distributors have been sharing over the years and find an even better practice because they realized that anything is possible.

To find what they needed, the innovation team at U.S. LBM looked to the airline industry.

Most of us are well-aware of the troubles and the challenges associated with the airline industry, which is often noted for its poor service. However, one area in which the airline industry excels is their ability to use technology to communicate to their customers.

Do you remember the days when you were making your flight arrangements and you had to be on hold with Delta or United for 30 minutes just to get the person on the phone? Today, of course, that's no longer the case. The airlines have come a long way in communicating with their customers.

Today, we can pull out our smartphones and open up an app to get that same information we used to wait half an hour for just a few years ago. Today, getting up-to-date information from an airline is much easier than any phone call and far more convenient than waiting 30 minutes. A tremendous amount of friction has been removed. U.S. LBM saw this and realized that, if it was possible for the airline industry, it must be possible for them as well.

> *To innovate successfully means we have to modify a concept to our industry, but in most cases, the heavy lifting has already been done.*

U.S. LBM crafted a vision and said, "Let's remove the friction in that ordering process. Let's remove the friction of our contractors knowing where and when their order is going to be delivered." It's important to note that U.S. LBM didn't have to reinvent the wheel. *They simply found what others had done to solve similar problems and brought it into their business!*

Of course, to innovate successfully means we have to

modify a concept to our industry, but in most cases, the heavy lifting has already been done. In this case, a mobile app allowed U.S. LBM to fundamentally change how it interacted with customers and improved the experience for everybody. All it took was the vision to see that these changes were possible, which led to U.S. LBM finding an existing solution from another industry.

ANYTHING IS POSSIBLE

Chapter 6
Distributors Have to Dream the Dream Again

When I was at the Fairmont Hotel in Washington a few years ago, I ran into Mike Medart, the president of Medart Inc. in St. Louis. As we were standing in the hotel lobby, our conversation turned to innovation and how distributors are reluctant to change. Mike said something amazing. He said, "Dirk, distributors have to dream the dream again." I thought this was brilliant. It was a simple, succinct quote that captures the "anything is possible" attitude. We just need to change our frame of reference and dare to dream.

What's great is we can get this kind of inspiration from anything. For instance, I'm a huge U2 fan. I think that U2 is one of the most creative rock and roll bands that's ever existed. Have you ever noticed that U2 doesn't sing about sex and rock and roll? They leave those areas for other bands to sing about. Instead, U2 sings about the future. They encourage us to dream about the world we want to live in. This is a terrific message not just for leaders, but humanity in general.

It's also a particularly great message for those of us in distribution. Dream of the type of business that you want to create, not today but tomorrow. Don't be afraid to go out to the world, to the industry, to your employee and dream aloud.

When you dream aloud, sometimes people are going to say you're crazy. Don't let their words stop you. Instead, think about what U2 says about the future and how our only limits are the limits of our imagination. If you want to drive innovation within your organization – which I believe is critically necessary throughout the distribution industry – you need to be in the vision business. You need to constantly think, dream, and imagine.

After you finish reading this essay, I want you to dream a little bit. Turn off your phone, turn off your email, get a journal, and start dreaming a little bit about that future.

Here are six questions you might want to ask yourself.

1. Where do you want to make a profound difference?

2. What do you want your organization to become? What do you want your culture, value proposition, and business model to become?

3. What would you achieve if you were ten times bolder? In distribution, we tend to be great when it comes to incremental work. However, it's time to think bolder. Think about the examples from the beginning of this essay when I suggested that

anything is possible from putting a man on the moon to driverless cars to completely new business models which provide that third daily activity (i.e., home, work and Starbucks).

4. What would you do if you were guaranteed to not fail? The technology that's available today is amazing. Yes, there's an investment. Yes, there are some unknowns. But what would you do with this technology if you were guaranteed to get a return on your investment?

5. Where will you lead your customers? I define innovation as leading our customers to a better future for which they are willing and capable of rewarding us. Where will you lead yours?

6. What is the future reality that you absolutely believe is possible through committed effort? You are in the vision business. Anything is possible. People are making the impossible possible every day. Think about it.

ANYTHING IS POSSIBLE

Chapter 7
Catalyze Change with The Visioning Spectrum

I want to share a model with you that will help you bring the concept of "anything is possible with vision" into your organization. I call this The Visioning Spectrum.

Good, bad, or indifferent, most distributors are managing their businesses for today. They're at the status quo on one side of the spectrum. Your business is likely among them. You most likely have a good business (and no doubt a profitable one), but you're managing it for today. On the other side of the spectrum is a disruptive future. By using your vision to look ahead to that future, you're preparing for it. As a leader in your organization, you must ensure that you aren't just innovating for today but are trying to be sustainable, relevant, and profitable in the future.

To do that, take stock of your current situation. Your management activities are driving certain levels of performance and that performance is driving results for your current generation of customers and employees. Look around your offices at your employees, and also look at your customers. You're performing to meet their current needs. However, as you move towards that other

The Visioning Spectrum

	Perform	Prioritize	Thrive	
	Today's Generation of Customers & Employees		Next Generation of Customers & Employees	
Status Quo	Managing For Today	Peer Into The Future	Innovating For The Future	Disruptive Future
				Relevance & Sustainability
	Activate Growth	Reduce Fog Of Uncertainty	Catalyze Change	
	Incremental		Transformational	

side of the spectrum, think about how you can innovate not just for your current customers and employees, but for that next generation of customers and employees.

Today, you're probably driving incremental changes. Most distributors look for a 2% or 3% improvement in their warehouses, through their sales activities and so on to drive incremental growth. If you want to bridge the gap from managing for today to innovating for the future, however, prioritize how you invest your resources and put into place a process for somehow seeing into the future. Remember, the future is already here, it's just not evenly distributed.

Have the discipline to continually ask, "Where must we drive this business? How must we innovate?" So much is going on at any one moment: Technology changes, government regulations, generational changes, varying business models, customer demands, and so on and so forth.

ANYTHING IS POSSIBLE

Chapter 8
Peering Into the Future

So what do we do? Where do we invest? What strategies do we invest in? Where do we innovate? What types of technology should we be bringing into our organizations? There are a lot of decisions to be made and a tremendous fog of uncertainty that needs to be cut through to make them. We reduce this fog by peering into the future. Our vision leads to our ability to catalyze real change – significant, transformational change – so we can innovate not just for today, but also for tomorrow.

When your organization is sitting in the middle of the spectrum – the area from which you can peer into the future – you will encounter a lot of uncertainty. To help manage this process, I recommend incorporating the following discipline within your organization which involves breaking up these questions to help your company prioritize and reduce the complexity of change. This involves dividing the issues into two categories.

In the first category, which makes up the bottom half of the equation, we have systemic shifts. These are disruptions or trends which are happening globally, economically, geo-politically, and technology-wise. All of these are outside of your control, but they will impact your business and customer service. It's important to identify these foundational, macro shifts and get a sense of where they're going.

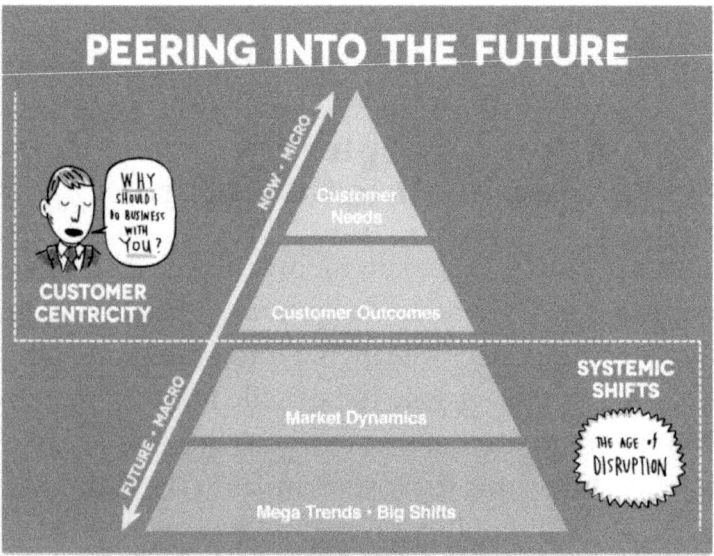

In the second category, which makes up the top half, figure out how these changes will impact your customers because innovation is about leading your customers to a better future in which they are willing and capable of rewarding you. Any major, systemic shift that affects your company will likewise impact your customers, so it's important to have sensors in place to identify and understand the previously mentioned mega trends.

From there, figure out how these trends are going to impact your company (or industry) so you can make judgments and informed decisions. Once you get past that level, start making informed decisions relative to how these trends are going to impact distribution.

Think about it not just from a distribution perspective, by the way, but also ask yourself, "How is this shift going to change the outcomes that our customers will be looking for? How will it change their desired outcomes regarding profitability and productivity? How will the demographic changes affect the availability of labor and our customers' ability to recruit labor?" Then, from there, begin looking into the day-to-day needs of your customers. Use this model of peering into the future to begin crafting your vision.

For an example of this model being put into practice, let's look at Chicago Tube & Iron, a distributor that deals in valves and fitting. Chicago Tube & Iron is notable for two very important reasons. First, the company has been around for over 100 years. In and of itself, this is a pretty impressive feat. However, secondly and more importantly, the company has been profitable for 100 consecutive years. Think about everything that our country and our economy has gone through in the past 100 years, including 17 recessions, depressions, the World Wars, Korea, Vietnam, and numerous other wars. Think about everything their suppliers and competitors have gone through in that same time. Yet somehow this company has managed to stay profitable even when almost everybody else hasn't. It's a truly remarkable accomplishment!

A lot of the credit belongs to Donald McNeely, the company's CEO. He's a brilliant individual, an amazing leader, a visionary, an innovator, and somebody who truly believes that anything is possible. What Don does on an ongoing basis is talk about the importance of inflection points. He thinks about that model of macro trends and market shifts. Doing so has helped Don to identify five core fundamental shifts which he keeps a careful eye on, which are:

- Demographic shifts, including millennials entering the market,

- The excess global capacity of steel, recognizing China has the ability to dump steel into the U.S.,

- Globalization and how we are now competing against companies across the world, impacting pricing,

- Non-product costs, such the cost of health care and regulations, and, finally

- How the internet is changing the way businesses operate.

Don has chosen to remove the complexity and fog of uncertainty by deciding to craft his business's vision around five fundamental shifts. It's this type of thinking that has led to 100 years of profitability at Chicago Tube & Iron. You can do this as well. You can create a sustainable, relevant future by determining your own focuses and then crafting your vision around them.

ANYTHING IS POSSIBLE

Chapter 9
Next Steps to Unleashing the Power Behind YOUR Vision

Everything I've talked about can be achieved within your own business because anything is possible through the power of vision. Best of all, you can start this process today. Begin by using the four practices above for changing your thinking and frame of reference.

> *What we want to become is far more important than our current state.*

Do this by bringing humility and hunger to your organization. Go out and share your point of view while acknowledging that you don't have all the answers. Whereas yesterday you may have thought that your opinion was the only one worth hearing, today you're going to recognize that other points of view could shine a light on something that you've missed or overlooked. Be open to having your point of view challenged and to questioning new points of view.

You can do this, too, by exploring new ideas which originate outside of your industry. Remember: If you use the same "best practices" that everybody else in your industry is using, you'll only achieve parity. Instead, look outside distribution for inspiration.

Move beyond your current network. It's important to make time in your calendar for different events where you can meet people outside of your current circles. This can lead to serendipitous encounters – like my meeting with Saul Kaplan on the deck of the U.S.S. George Washington – with individuals who can radically change your vision.

Consider attending the UnleashWD Summit where you'll encounter speakers from other industries who can introduce you to new ideas and new ways of thinking. You may find that they've discovered solutions to problems similar to ones in your organization or, in some cases, problems you hadn't even noticed!

Explore the future. Take the Visioning Spectrum and apply that model to your business. Use the Peering Into the Future framework and ask yourself, "Am I systemically peering into the future? What gaps are there in terms of my ability to craft my vision? What do I need to get better?" By setting up sensors to detect changes, you can prepare your business for trends before they hit your company or industry.

Finally, I want to leave you with one last story. Several months ago, I was invited down to Dallas to be the keynote speaker at a multi-day meeting for about 230 of Hajoca's sales and showroom team members. Also speaking at the event was Rick Fantham, the company's CEO, who kicked things off with a speech about possibility, including the possibilities that could come from this meeting. Most importantly, he asked his team to adopt a possibility mindset.

All too often in our organizations, we want to beat down unproven ideas. We want to attack ideas that don't demonstrate a return on investment. We want to be pulled back to the status quo. I ask that you abandon those bad habits and instead take Rick's advice by adopting a possibility mindset. I hope that you'll use the tools and practices that you've learned here to craft and execute a vision for your own organization, and I sincerely hope that I've convinced you that anything is possible through the power of vision. I look forward to the stories that you'll someday tell me about the success you found within your own organization after making use of your vision.

About the Author

William Taylor, Co-Founder of Fast Company magazine said of Dirk: "Every field has its rabble rousers, change agents, thought leaders-people with the wisdom to understand the past, and the creativity to conjure up a new vision for the future. In the field of wholesale distribution, Dirk Beveridge is that thought leader."

As one of the country's most outstanding speakers in the distribution industry, Dirk delivers a new voice, a new energy, and a new outlook.

Dirk's custom tailored presentations deliver original, proven, and often disruptive thinking. His energy and passion for excellence are infectious and inspire audiences to step from the zone of comfort to unleash the urgency of change. Beveridge is routinely asked to speak on innovation, business strategy, sales, and leadership.

As an entrepreneur Beveridge noticed that innovation was bypassing distributors, and so he founded

UnleashWD in 2012 which is setting a bold agenda for over 300,000 distribution businesses. This one-of-a-kind and essential summit has helped hundreds already by delivering an outstanding immersive experience through amazing speakers, inspired networking and relevant tools.

For over 30 years as a consultant to a wide range of companies, Beveridge has helped leading firms align, focus, and strengthen their sales and leadership strategies to remain relevant, outperform the market, and provide deeper value to customers.

Visit www.DirkBeveridge.com for more information.

Other Publications and Programs by Dirk Beveridge

Keynotes – Executive Retreats – Workshops

Dirk Beveridge knows your audience is desperate to find new ways to significantly separate themselves and their company in a rapidly changing market. How can your people create a culture of innovation and discover new ideas that will grow your company for tomorrow … and today? As the industry authority on leading innovation, Dirk has answers and teaches how your leaders can innovate now. His passionate and energy-infused presentations unleash your team's talent and creativity to generate new value growth and profits.

Visit www.DirkBeveridge.com to book Dirk for your next corporate event.

UnleashWD
The Only Innovation Summit For Distributors

Each fall Dirk curates and produces UnleashWD, the only innovation summit for distributors and their supply chain partners. The UnleashWD Summit is where the most driven and creative leaders discover innovative solutions to profitably and confidently seize the future.

Visit www.UnleashWD.com for more information about the next UnleashWD Summit.

Weekly Podcast Show

In this weekly podcast show, Dirk Beveridge sits down with some of the most brilliant leaders and innovators from within distribution and beyond. Each guest is successfully innovating and changing the way business is done, and shares their secrets of success through a series of interesting and informative interviews. They have chosen to be the disrupter rather than the disrupted. The Innovative Distributor™ framework serves as the context for each

CEO series of five podcast episodes, allowing Dirk to go deep with the innovators you want to learn from.

You can find, subscribe and listen to Innovate! For the Future on iTunes or by visiting www.DirkBeveridge.com/podcast.

Latest Industry Research

Dirk's best-selling book *INNOVATE! How Successful Distributors Lead Change in Disruptive Times* has been called, "Indispensable," "A must read," and "One of the best business books I have ever read" by several CEOs throughout the distribution industry. Writing about *INNOVATE!*, former Supreme Allied Commander at NATO, Admiral James Stavridis (Ret), observed: "At the heart of any healthy industry is innovation -- the ability to change as circumstances dictate with agility and intelligence.

In *INNOVATE!*, Dirk Beveridge provides a roadmap for creating innovation. This is an instant classic and has wide applicability not only in the complex world of distribution, but in the widest sense."

Learn more about this research project at www.DirkBeveridge.com/research.

Digital Courses

Innovation Inspired is a turn-key, cloud-based training program that shows distribution executives how to impact real change in their company. This 6-part course delivers a streamlined, systematized experience for your entire executive team through thought-provoking, energized, to-the-point video modules that team members can absorb and be inspired by.

Each module contains accompanying tools including worksheets, roadmaps, and a stimulating series of questions that act as catalysts for discussions that will lead to innovation and support real action in your distribution company.

Innovation Inspired allows you to impact real change without leaving your office, spending a fortune, or having to figure out how to translate your vision into an actionable plan. It's all done for you in this successful new program. Visit InnovationInspired.DirkBeveridge.com to get more information on the latest release of this program.

White Papers

Distribution leaders find themselves in a once-in-a-career opportunity to create a culture of change, transformation and innovation. The Innovative Distributor™ is a complimentary white paper written by Dirk Beveridge that provides a path to catalyze your organization to sustained relevancy.

Download your copy of **The Innovative Distributor** at www.DirkBeveridge.com/the-innovative-distributor.

Other Essays in this Series

This essay is the first of several coming soon that are the result of a dynamic series of workshop-style presentations Dirk recently delivered entitled *5 Weeks of Innovation Unleashed*.

Throughout the series, Dirk delivers true 'roll-up-your-sleeves and get it done' action items that distribution leaders can apply NOW to begin changing their business to meet the innovative needs necessary to stay competitive TODAY, in the age of disruption. No matter where you sit on the spectrum of innovation, each essay in the series delivers eye-opening case studies, step-by-step processes to follow, catalytic questions to ask yourself and your team to launch you into action, and most importantly, a clear path to follow, already blazed by some of the most innovative, most successful distributors in our lifetime.

As a leader, it's your responsibility to keep your organization motivated and competitive. What Dirk includes in this powerful new series will deliver the tools for exactly that. Stay tuned in for more information!

> ***Join our mailing list*** to receive our cutting edge videos, eBooks, podcasts and more, all tailored to the distribution industry. Simply visit **dirkbeveridge.com** to learn how.

Anything is Possible